Start Your Own

INDIE

Publishing

Company!

Everything You Need to Know!

K Kelly McElroy

Start Your Own Indie Publishing Company — Everything You Need To Know © 2015

by K Kelly McElroy.

For information contact: info@uptownmediaventures.com

Book and Cover design by Team Uptown

ISBN: 978-1-68121-022-3

10 9 8 7 6 5 4 3 2 1

Dedicated to my literary friends and family and all the literary minded people out there!

Page left intentionally blank

Testimonials

"I literally was about to spend nearly $3,000 trying to get my two books published, *Holy Terror* and *Oh the Shame!*. However, I talked with K Kelly and he told me that he would publish BOTH books for me for free. To my surprise, after I expressed the desire to start my own publishing company, he told me that he would give me a free copy of this book, in exchange for my testimonial. All I can say is that this book was EVERYTHING I dreamed of and more!!!! I now have everything in place for my new indie publishing company. I am eternally thankful for this extremely valuable information!"

Ritchie Mac

Author of Holy Terror and Oh the Shame!

CEO Freedom Underground Publishing

"Everything I expected and more! This book is a treasure trove of information and has saved me a great deal of time and money!"

Jeff Mixon

Author of Save Our Souls Volumes 1 and 2

Table of Contents

Introduction

I, like many of you who are reading this book, wasted a lot of time and energy searching the internet and getting sucked into various deceptive self-publishing advertisements.

After they get you to sign up onto their website, they started reeling you in as a very eager author; who just wants to get your words out to the world!

What started out as maybe free or a $199 self-publishing plan morphed into a $1,500, $2,500, $3,500, or even more expensive plan! I knew that there had to be a better way...

So I travailed all the information and misinformation I could get my hands on. It became apparent that most of it was the horse chasing the carrot which, for some odd reason, the horse NEVER got to eat - unless he paid an exorbitant fee!

Eventually, I started to see things between the angles and the scene became increasingly clear over time. The result? Starting an indie publishing company from my home with an investment of less than $3,000 (less than I would have ultimately paid one of those slick indie self-publishing companies just to get one title published!).

At the time of the writing of this book, my publishing company *Uptown Media Joint Ventures* (which is barely a year old) has over 25 titles in print and I have not looked back. The experience has been very challenging, yet very rewarding, as well.

What To Expect From This Book

1. All the basic information required to start an indie publishing company.

2. All the hardware and software requirements to start an indie publishing company.

3. General guidelines for editing books.

4. General guidelines for book layout and book cover design to publish a professional quality publication.

What NOT To Expect From This Book

1. EVERY technical detail for book editing.

2.   EVERY technical detail for book layout and book cover design.

3.   Marketing advice or schemes to get a million copies of your book sold.

The simple goal of this book is to assist the reader with ALL the necessary information needed to get an indie publishing company started, with the capability of growing into a significant enterprise.

This book does not attempt to tell the reader how they can become indie publishing millionaires. This book will present no misleading claims. Marketing tactics are left totally up to the soon-to-be publisher.

After reading this book, you WILL have ALL the information needed to start your own indie publishing company. As with anything else in life, the rest is up to the individual.

Wishing great success to all the literary minded people in the world!

Peace, Joy & Love

K Kelly McElroy

Page left intentionally blank

Introductory Matters

(Publishing Industry Overview)

Traditional Publishing

In traditional publishing, the author completes his or her manuscript, writes a query letter or a proposal, and submits these documents to a publishing house (or has a literary agent do this for them, if one can be acquired). An editor reads it, considers whether it is right for the house, and decides either to reject it (leaving the author free to offer it to another publisher) or to publish it. If the publishing house decides to publish the book, the house buys the rights from the writer and pays him or her an advance on future royalties. The house puts up the money to design and package the book, prints as many copies of the book as it thinks will sell, markets the book, and finally distributes the finished book to the public.

Indie or Self-Publishing

The process is a bit different for self-publishing. An author who decides to self-publish basically becomes the publisher. The author must proofread the final text and provide the funds required to publish the book, as well as the camera-ready artwork. The author is responsible for marketing and distributing the book, filling orders, and running advertising campaigns. In the past, the author had to decide on the number of copies to print, sometimes resulting in stacks of unsold books gathering dust in the garage! Fortunately, the Print on Demand (POD) technology now used by some self-publishing companies means that authors can have fewer copies printed—only as many as they need, in fact.

The Differences Between The Two

With traditional publishing, a manuscript can take years to become a book. First, an author may have to pitch the manuscript to several publishing houses before it is picked up. Considering that the bigger houses can take up to six months to work through the "slush pile" (the multitude of queries on editors' desks) to get to your manuscript and that you will likely have to try several publishing houses before you get one to show interest. That's a lot of waiting! Then, if a house does decide to take your book, the actual process of producing the book takes at least another year. Admittedly, this process applies mainly to fiction. Nonfiction books that are topical and relevant to current world events might be pushed through more quickly.

With self-publishing, depending on the company, an author can literally have a finished book—hardcover or paperback or both - in his or her hands within six months. And, with the advent of eBooks, this can be reduced to weeks, or even days. Of course, authors have to pay for this service, which raises the issue of money.

Dollars and Sense?

With self-publishing, you often pay thousands of dollars, depending on the company you choose. In contrast, with traditional publishing, you are paid an advance, ranging from small sums to seven-digit figures. In traditional publishing, the publishing house usually has huge resources, experience, knowledge, and contacts. They may vigorously promote your book. When you self-publish, you pay for everything - design, editing, printing, advertising, distribution - to get your book into stores and ultimately into people's hands. You're all by yourself; self-publishing works best for people who are good at self-marketing. The major payoff for all of your payout, though, is control.

Power and Control

Publishers might refuse to publish a book because it is too controversial, doesn't fit into a niche, or because they don't think the book will sell. Often an author's joy at selling a manuscript turns into despair when an editor at a publishing house completely alters that manuscript into a whole different narrative. With self-publishing, the author has much greater control over the contents, design, and appearance, as well as where the book is marketed and distributed.

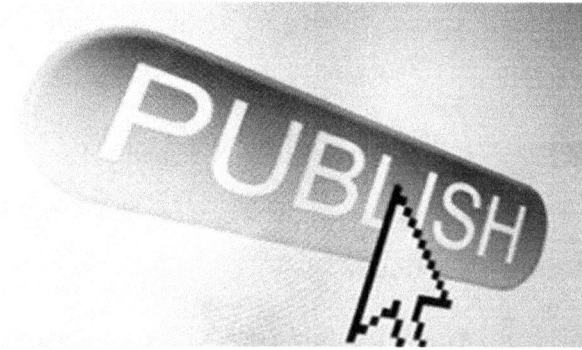

Traditional Publishing Positives

- Most offer an advance, sometimes a large one

- Wide distribution and more exposure

- They do the editing, formatting, cover art

- Marketing power

Traditional Publishing Negatives

- It is hard to get a traditional publishing deal

- Difficult to implement changes

- The traditional publisher retains the control over art, the title, and even the content at times

- Don't use the marketing power they wield effectively

- Royalties are usually paid twice a year

- Don't involve you in many of the decisions regarding your book

- EBooks prices are usually too costly

- The standard royalty rates are low, between 6% and 25%

- Publication usually takes six to eighteen months

<u>Self-Publishing Positives</u>

- Almost anyone can do it

- You are usually paid every month

- Very good royalty rates

- It's easy to make changes to book

- You retain major control of your work

- You control price and cover

- Fast publication process

Self-Publishing Negatives

- Less sales potential

- No free professional editing, formatting, or cover art

- The indie book market is much smaller than the traditional market

- Self-publishing still has an inferior comparative reputation

Every person has their own criteria and goals and one size does not fit all.

Publishing as a Business

Becoming a publisher can be as simple or as complicated as one can make it. However, there are various requirements that are mandatory to be considered a publisher.

ISBN (International Standard Book Numbers)

One of the main criteria is for the publisher to own its own ISBN (International Standard Book Number) numbers. These ISBN number can be purchased only from a privately held company - **R.R. Bowker**.

There is a charge that varies depending upon the number of ISBNs purchased, with prices starting at $125.00 for a single number. The more numbers purchased, the cheaper the ISBN numbers become. As of the printing of this study guide, 100 ISBN can be purchased from R.R. Bowker for $500 ($5 each) and 1,000 ISBN can be purchased for $1,500 ($1.50 each).

Legal Formalities

There is no requirement to establish your publishing company as any specific legal entity. The scope of this study guide does not go into any detail of entity options such as sole-proprietorship, corporations, limited liability companies (llc), along with a host of other types of entities. There are many resources on the internet that can be referenced for direction.

Bank Account and Tax Verification

If a person, or group of people, expects to be paid as a publisher, a legitimate bank account has to be in existence and they are required to submit tax information relating to themselves or their business entity.

Depending on the distributor, they may require bank account and routing numbers. Some distributors use secured payment services like *PayPal*.

Contracts

Royalties and Payments
y to the Author a royalty as a percentage of net revenues accru
described above in (1a) according to the following schedule.
either as a percentage of retail sales of the Author's Work
nue realized by wholesale on-selling of the Wor

If the publisher plans on publishing the works of others, then the publisher should have standard form contract(s) that fit the needs of authors who choose to have their manuscripts published as books through the publisher's company.

Other potential contractual relationship may involve book distributors, editors and/or graphic designers.

Relating to potential authors, who may come on board, it is best to spell out EXACTLY what your services entail and what they should expect from your company. Many authors expect the same treatment from an indie publisher as from a traditional publisher. Of course, most indie companies do not have the same resources as the large traditional publishers this should be made very clear.

In most cases the author should be plainly told through word of mouth and company documents that they are ultimately responsible for editing and marketing their book. The indie publisher is simply taking a cut of any profits derived from the sale of the book.

Make sure you make no misleading representations to potential authors! You will be sorry if you do so!

Web Sites

If a publisher decides to direct sell books, for instance, the publisher may want a website (which is not always necessary). This book does not go into the details of website development for a publisher. However, the publisher should ensure that their site is user friendly and that transactions can be performed with ease. **Do your homework before you use a web hosting company. Some have quality and service issues!**

Copyrights

What is copyright?

Copyright is a form of protection grounded in the U.S. Constitution and granted by law for original works of authorship fixed in a tangible medium of expression. Copyright covers both published and unpublished works.

It is recommended that an author obtain a copyright for literary works even though a copyright registration is not technically required. A Copyright exists from the moment the work is created. You will have to register, however, if you wish to bring a lawsuit for infringement of a U.S. work. See Circular 1, Copyright Basics, section "Copyright Registration."

Why should I register my work if copyright protection is automatic?

Registration is recommended for a number of reasons. Many choose to register their works because they wish to have the facts of their copyright on the public record and have a certificate of registration. Registered works may be eligible for statutory damages and attorney's fees in successful litigation. Finally, if registration occurs within 5 years of publication, it is considered prima facie evidence in a court of law.

If you do not have your manuscript copyrighted, Uptown can obtain one for you upon submission of your manuscript. For further information about copyright and the fee to obtain a copyright, check out the United States Copyright Office's website at www.copyright.gov./

Income Possibilities and Royalties

The Advance

In most cases with traditional publishing, if you are writing your first book, you can expect to get an advance of 2,500 to $10,000. The key thing to remember about that advance is that it's an advance, so you have to pay that money back. And if it's your first book, you are less likely to get a big advance.

Also, you as the author should be prepared to be fully involved in marketing your book! It should not be expected that the traditional publisher, or any publisher, will invest significant sums into a marketing plan specifically for your book.

Royalties Off Books Sales

In most cases, publishers will offer you a contract where you get 10-15% royalties off each sale. Now there is a big qualification to this number. Some publishers will offer you that rate off list price (Gross royalties), and some will offer you that rate off the amount of profit they make off the book (net royalties). The net amount is typically 50% of the book's price.

So for example, if a book as a list price of $25.00, that means that if your contract says you get 10% royalties off list, then you will get $2.50 per book. If you are getting 10% of net profits, then you'd get around $1.25 per book. Most publishers seem to prefer to offer net royalties.

Additionally, you will likely get a higher royalty rate for eBooks, plus you may be offered a higher royalty rate as your sales of the book increase. You should ask the publisher for both.

For example, if you get a $2,500 advance for your book and you get a 10% royalties net profit, and the book's list price is $20.00. That means you are making $1.00 per book. You will need to sell 2,500 copies of your book just to break even. The points is that you will likely never make a penny from royalties off sales of your book (what the term "earn out" means). The average US non-fiction book sells about 250 copies a year and around 3,000 copies over its lifetime.

It's best to be liked by many, many people when you are an author!

Self-Publishing or Indie Publishing

The royalty rates for self or indie publishing are much higher than traditional publishing (usually 50 to 85% as opposed to 10 to 15%).

Also, the author retains substantial control of the her or his book. Any needed changes, updates, or alterations can be made fairly easy and efficiently.

The drawbacks are that there will be no Advance payment made and there is far less likelihood to get your book sold in a traditional "brick and mortar" book store. Many authors can be commercially successful even without having their book sold at a physical book store.

Distribution Channels

BARNES&NOBLE amazon.com
BOOKSELLERS

Most "indie," as opposed to traditionally, published books are sold on-line, as opposed to book stores, which is becoming somewhat of a dying breed – especially for the younger generations. Thus, an indie publishing company does not focus on sales in traditional book stores (of course if a book generates enough interest – the traditional book sellers will come-a-calling!).

An advantage to focusing on online retail book sales is that it is much less expensive and generates higher income streams, which benefit both the author and the publisher!

Barnes & Noble.com and *Amazon.com* are the preeminent online book retailers. However, there are plenty of alternatives in this internet age.

<u>Marketing</u>

The author must have an ACTIVE share in the marketing of a newly published book. An author cannot depend on a publisher to get the "word out" and generate interest in your book.

There are marketing tools out there now which include, but are not limited to:

The aforementioned social networking sites, along with many other sites, too numerous to detail in this book, should be exploited to your advantage. Gather as large an audience as you can to your social networking sites.

Ask friends to make reviews on your Amazon.com book site (and purchase your book of course) and share your sites with as many others as they can. Post links to your social network sites, as well.

There are many other processes too numerous to delineate in this book. Upon the publication of your book, you must be persistent in publicizing your book and keeping pace with innovations in technology on the World Wide Web along with other social networking opportunities.

1

Choosing a Business Name

To Be Or Not To Be
PUBLISHING

Before we can leave the gate en route to becoming the owner of an indie publishing company, we need a name. A name that separates your indie publishing company from a host of other established indie publishing companies.

It is best to try to be innovative without being off-putting. Reach inside your own psyche and develop your company name based on your values and sentiments – all with an eye to what would be enticing to others.

Remember that the name of your company is a reflection of you and your ideals. It should not have a cookie cutter feel or be trite or banal. This same principle also applies to your logo(s) that will be used with your business cards, advertisements, web-site, along with other potential uses.

The name of your publishing company and the look of your logo should not remind anyone of any other entity or brand, except yours!

Logo Design

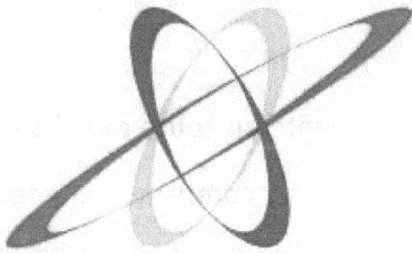

MY LOGO

It is best to design a logo in advance of operating your publishing company so that you will have it already made for use on your business cards, books, and web-site (if you so choose).

Again, as brought out earlier, your logo should not have a cookie cutter feel or be trite or banal and it should not remind anyone of any other entity or brand.

There are many logo design software programs out there like: ***Sothink Logo Maker***, ***Eximious Soft Logo Designer***, ***Logo Design Studio***, along with a host of many other programs.

These programs can cost from as low as $20 to $200 and higher.

2

ISBNs and Metadata

ISBN 978-1-4116-8691-5

90000 >

9 781411 686915

No one can start a legitimate indie publishing company without owning ISBN numbers for your book titles. One of the main criteria is for the publisher to own its own ISBN (International Standard Book Number) numbers. These ISBN number can be purchased only from one privately held company - R.R. Bowker.

Bowker. | Identifier Services

There is a charge that varies depending upon the number of ISBNs purchased, with prices starting at

$125.00 for a single number (which makes little to no sense whatsoever).

The more numbers purchased, the cheaper the ISBN numbers become. As of the printing of this book, 100 ISBN can be purchased from R.R. Bowker for $500 ($5 each) and 1,000 ISBN can be purchased for $1,500 ($1.50 each).

R.R. Bowker has a monopoly on the issuance of these ISBN numbers (why? I do not have a clue), so it is always best to invest in these numbers as early as possible before they go up in price. I got caught like that because I waited too long to purchase my ISBN numbers. The price went up from $1,000 for 1,000 ISBNs to $1,500 for 1,000 ISBNs, when I finally purchased mine. OUCH!

Besides selling ISBNs, R.R. Bowker sells ISBN Barcodes and a host of other publishing related services. At the time of the writing of this book, R.R. Bowker charges $25 for the barcode which is ridiculously expensive!

The best route is to make your own barcode images (if necessary because maybe you are doing the actual printing, for example). For publisher's purposes, the production of barcode is unnecessary because you will be submitting your work to **_Amazon's Createspace_** or

Ingram's Lightning Source, for example, and they do all that stuff for you.

However, If you do print your own publications then there are several barcode software production programs that you can purchase and never have to pay for them ever again!

There are many barcode programs like *BC Studio*, *Barcode Generator*, *Easy Barcode Creator*, along with many others. These programs range in price from free to several hundred dollars. The key is to make sure that the program makes ISBN book barcodes.

R.R. Bowker is not all bad because they have a great free service called *Bowker Link®* that is a great tool to get your books on *Barnes & Noble.com* without having to go through their byzantine processes (more on that topic is discussed in Chapter 8, Book Submission).

Some Information Regarding Metadata

There is a quite a bit of information that is required to submit a book for listing to on-line resellers such as Amazon.com or Barnes & Noble.com or other major book distributors. For example, an International Standard Book Number (ISBN), as previously mentioned in this study guide, is required to have your book listed with any major book seller or distributor. An ISBN is a unique numeric commercial book identifier based upon a 13-digit Standard Book Numbering (SBN) code.

The graphic above illustrates what a bar code for a book would look like on the back cover of the book that you will publish. It should be noted that the BISAC (Book Industry Subject and Category) is a cataloguing system that is set to replace the Dewey Decimal System for cataloging books.

<u>Information that is usually required to be submitted to an on-line seller or book distributor includes</u>:

1) The book's ISBN.

2) Title of Book.

3) Author's Name.

4) Publisher name (for example - ***Uptown Media Joint Ventures***).

5) Format (i.e. hard cover, trade paperback, e-Book, etc... It should be noted that each type of book format requires a separate ISBN).

6) Price (Discussed by the author and the publisher).

7) Publication date (Provided by publisher).

8) BISAC Audience (Submitted by publisher).

9) BISAC Subject (Submitted by publisher).

10) Discount offered to the reseller and/or distributor.

Other data that should be available for submission include:

1. Author Bio

2. Book Overview

3. Editorial Reviews

4. Key Words for Searches

Keywords and metadata help search engines at Amazon (and elsewhere) do what the ancient librarians of Alexandria did: help readers find the books they're interested in. Adding a variety of carefully selected keywords to your title, subtitle, book description, tags and categories as well as to the actual text inside your book will make a big difference—often giving your book first or second page placement in Amazon results rather than several screens later. It's surprising how many authors don't put much effort into keyword selection.

Where Does the Metadata Go?

So where do indie authors use this metadata? All over the place—especially in databases such as Bowker's and with retailers such as *Amazon*, *Kobo*, *Nook* and *iBooks*. Incidentally, whoever purchases your ISBN from R.R. Bowker is listed as the publisher and controls the book's metadata so we always suggest you buy your own ISBN from R.R. Bowker's identifier services page.

Once you've done that you can log-in, click on your ISBN number and start to supply your metadata by filling out the full title detail form using as many specific-to-your-book keywords as possible.

3.

Registering Your Business

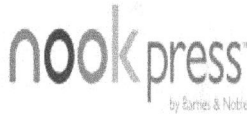

createspace **BARNES&NOBLE**
www.bn.com

IngramSpark

Lightning Source

amazonkindle

nookpress
by Barnes & Noble

So now you OWN your OWN ISBNs that are assigned to YOUR indie publishing company. It feels great! Doesn't it? But, really this is just the beginning of a significant process.

However, you are reading this book. Smart move! Why? Because you just saved yourself a bunch of waited time, energy, and money!

This next step of registering your publishing company is just as important as buying your ISBN numbers. An indie publishing company must set up an account with every entity that she or he wishes to publish through.

Generally speaking, the process is not usually unduly time-consuming.

> **It should be noted that there is no specific legal formation required to start your publishing company like incorporation, LLC, Scorp, etc. It can be simply a sole proprietorship. The choice is up to the individual.**
>
> **SEEK A LOCAL TAX ACCOUNTANT OR ATTORNEY FOR ADVICE ON WHAT'S BEST FOR YOU**

The information needed to register an account for your indie publishing company for *Createspace*, for example, is fairly straightforward:

1. E-mail address
2. First and last names
3. Your country

It's just that simple to create an account for most self-publishing distributors. It gets somewhat more involved when you set up your account to get paid royalties. The information required to set up your account to get paid royalties generally includes:

1. First and last names

2. Social Security number or your company EIN number

3. Bank account information

4. Tax ID verification (this is done internally by the distributor)

There are options as to where you can have your royalties forwarded including a typical bank account, a physical check, or a PayPal account. It should be noted that most distributors will only submit a "hard check" if a certain dollar amount of sales is obtained.

The aforementioned aspects of starting your own indie publishing company are fairly straightforward, so now we will continue on to other necessary considerations.

4

Hardware

A publisher should have the best and fastest equipment that she or he can afford to make the publishing process flow as efficiently as possible.

Computer(s) with sufficient RAM and hard drive memory is critical. The computer(s) (preferably two systems) must be equipped with the appropriate software as will be discussed in the Software section of this book.

The minimum suggested RAM is at least four (4) gigabytes (however, the more RAM, the better). The minimum suggested hard drive space is 500 gigabytes.

Also, the system should have a minimum of three to four USB ports for USB memory sticks or external hard drives; and at least two LAN ports for wired internet connections. Of course, a USB wireless internet adapter can be used as an alternative.

It is imperative to backup all your documents in more than one location. Therefore, you must have external USB drives (either flash or external drives) to back up your documents!

Of course a publisher must have suitable office equipment like ergonomically appropriate desks and chairs. You should be as comfortable and efficient as possible – it makes a huge difference!

In starting out, a new indie publisher can probably get away with spending $1,000 to $1,500 on computer(s) with the requisite capacity.

5

Software

Word Processing

The Holy Grail of word processing is, for better or worse, *Microsoft® Word*. It's as necessary for the efficient production of a manuscript as oxygen and water is for human life. There are so many "bells and whistles" to this software that it would take literally years to master every single function available.

Fortunately for us, it does not take an extensive knowledge base to successfully write and format a book in Word. However, it takes some skill and practice to achieve the requisite level of expertise. Word can cost from $80 for Word only to $110 for *Microsoft® Office*.

REMEMBER

PRACTICE,

PRACTICE,

AND MORE PRACTICE!

Is required to become proficient with any software program.

Keep At It!

Conversion

In most applications, a manuscript must be delivered to a printer in either a Word document format (doc. or docx.) or if a PDF format.

Portable Document Format (PDF) is a file format used to present documents in a manner independent of application software, hardware, and operating systems. Each PDF file encapsulates a complete description of a fixed-layout flat document, including the text, fonts, graphics, and other information needed to display it.

The vast majority of text or document files downloaded on the internet today are in the PDF format. Thus it is essential to have a newer Word program that can convert Word files into PDF files. Based on this, it is imperative for a writer to have not only the basic Adobe Acrobat Reader, but Acrobat Professional, as well.

Acrobat Professional allows the user to convert PDF files into other formats, like JPEG, HTML, Word, and many other file types. The basic Acrobat Reader does not have this conversion function which is necessary for many applications in forwarding various types of documents for publishing.

Cover Design

This is where many, who have enough technical skill to produce the interior of a book, fall short. The technical aspect of book cover design is discussed in the Book Cover Design and Technical Aspects section of this book.

As with Microsoft Word, in the word processing arena, Adobe's Photo Shop is the Holy Grail when it comes to graphic design, including the design of book covers. Photo Shop is, arguably, much more technically complex that Word. Many authors who choose to self-publish wind up paying significant money to have a professional graphic designer make their book covers.

However, if a person has the aptitude and patience to learn most of the basic functions, it is more than worthwhile to learn as much as possible about the vast features found in Photoshop. Photoshop software is very pricey. The one I use Photoshop CS6 retails for $700.

Note: one the best free paint and photo programs, that really is better than most paid software, is the Paint.Net software.

Other Software

ISBN 978-1-4116-8691-5

90000 >

9 781411 686915

If you want to go all-out then there is software that allows an author and/or publisher to create their own bar codes with their own ISBN (International Standard Book Number) numbers. Some of the available software includes: Bar Code Generator, BC Studio, and Easy Bar Code.

6

Book Layout Rules

There really are not too many book layout rules. The predominate book layout rules are as follows:

- **Left hand side pages can be blank, but right hand side pages should ALMOST ALWAYS show content** in your book. As with any rule, there is a caveat. For instance, I did a compilation book with all of the author's pictures included before their articles. To accommodate this, I made sure the author's picture was always on the left hand side page. So sometimes, in this case, a right hand side page would be left blank because an article stopped on a left hand side page. So I simply started the following article by putting the next author's picture on the following left hand side page.

- **A page with no text on it, generally, should NEVER have a page number** (there are exceptions as discussed below). Also, do not show page numbers on your title page, your copyright page, or any other page before the page AFTER your first chapter (this is because the first page in any Chapter NEVER has the page number on it). These are amateur mistakes. **Remember Chapters ALMOST ALWAYS begin on a right hand side page.**

- **Even-numbered pages should ALWAYS be on the left hand side of a book and vice versa.** Thus, obviously, the odd-numbered pages should ALWAYS be on the right hand side of a book. This rule MUST NEVER BE BROKEN. There are no caveats to this rule!

- With running heads, (the wording at the top of the page), where you put the chapter name or the author's name or the book title; if you have a blank page with no text on it, that page should be completely blank (that means **no running heads should be on a blank page**; there is an exception discussed below).

- Justifying means making the right edge of the type column straight, just like the left edge is. Some people set books with what we call "rag right," with the right side of the column ragged because the lines aren't adjusted to be the same length.

That's a really bad look for a book and you shouldn't do it. Sometimes you could do that for artistic effect but it is not recommended. **Generally, ALL book interiors should be justified**.

If you, carefully, adhere to the aforementioned book layout rules, your book likely will actually look the way it's supposed to look.

However, you know the old adage – rules are made to be broken. So the page number rule that applies to novels and the like may not apply to other types of books like poetry books, for example. I tried to follow the page numbering rule when I was laying out a poetry book and it was too unseemly. The poems were both long and sort and following the generally accepted page numbering rule made the book look haphazard; so I put a page number on every page.

A publisher should not just blindly follow book layout rules. These types of decision must be made with a view to the content of each individual book.

7

Book Layout
Technical Aspects

Choice of Book Formats

$\mathbf{Y}$ou, as the author, have the option of getting your book published in a hard copy format, in an e-Book format or both! The choice is yours!

Hard Copy or E-Book

Hard copy simply means a physical book as opposed to an e-Book. There are many publishing options for authors as far as the type and size of a hard copy book.

<u>The Most Prevalent Hard Copy Book Sizes Include:</u>

- ➢ 6-x-9 inches
- ➢ 8½-x-11 inches
- ➢ 5½-x-8½ inches
- ➢ 7-x-10 inches

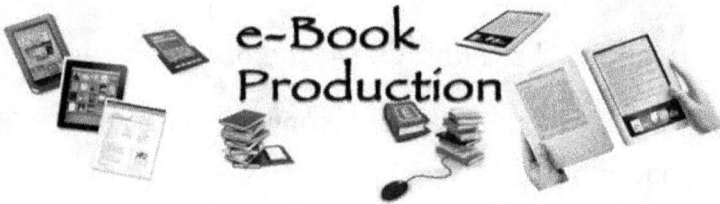

The publishing guidelines for E-Books vary greatly between each e-book retail distributor. Some want a book submitted in PDF, while other's want a Word or other type of document. The book cover requirements for E-Books vary greatly as well.

One of the most popular e-book distributors is Smashwords. They are somewhat of a renegade in the industry for people who either don't like or don't want to deal with the established indie distributors. I personally don't use them because they are exclusively for e-books and they have a byzantine process for title submission.

Formatting a 6 x 9 Inch Book

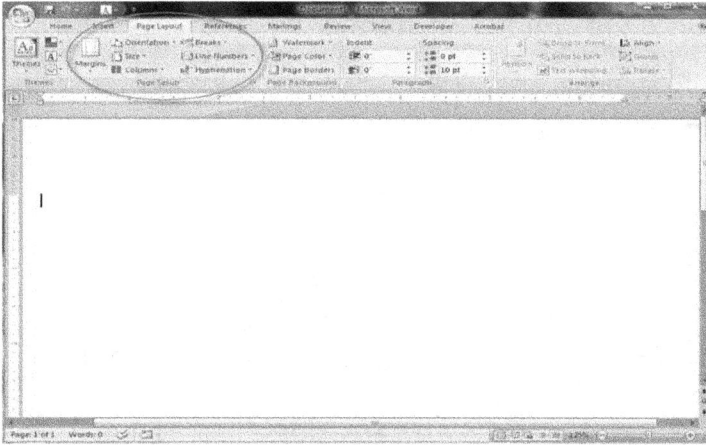

Most books are published using Microsoft Word, as will be discussed later in the Software Requirements section of this book. The guide lines change, but the rationale stays the same, for different book sizes. For our purposes we will discuss the margin requirements for the most widely published paperback book size – 6 x 9 inches.

It is not required that the writer write her or his manuscript in particular format because it is a fairly simple process to convert an 8 ½ x 11 inch Word document into the format required for a 6 x 9 inch book, for example. So **just write the book and format it later!**

Page Layout

Once the writer gets started with formatting his or her book, there are several areas they will need to examine. Primarily, Margins and Paper Size.

A Suggestion Regarding Page Numbering and Headers:

Prior to typing your book, it is recommended by most in the publishing world to add your page numbers or your headers. If you add them later, it can disrupt other formatting preferences you might have.

Personally, I do this after I write the book, then I set the margins, and last I do the page numbering first, then the headers.

To insert these, please visit **Insert** and view the available **header** and **footer** options. It is common to include a header at the top and a page number in the bottom or footer area.

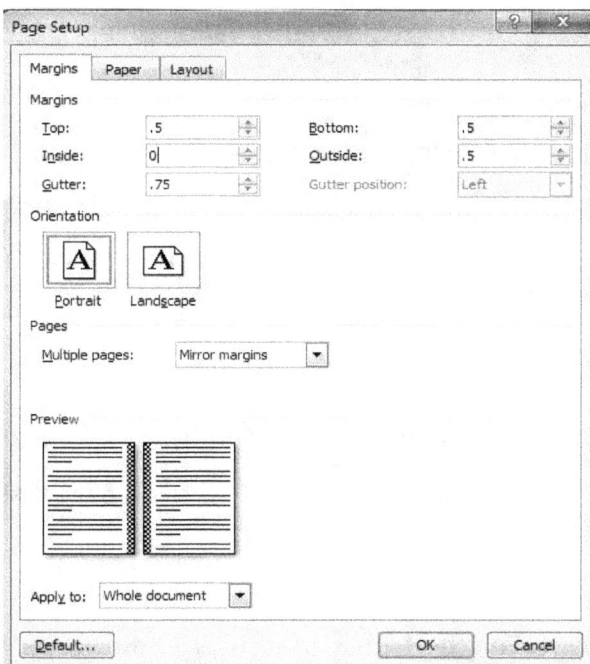

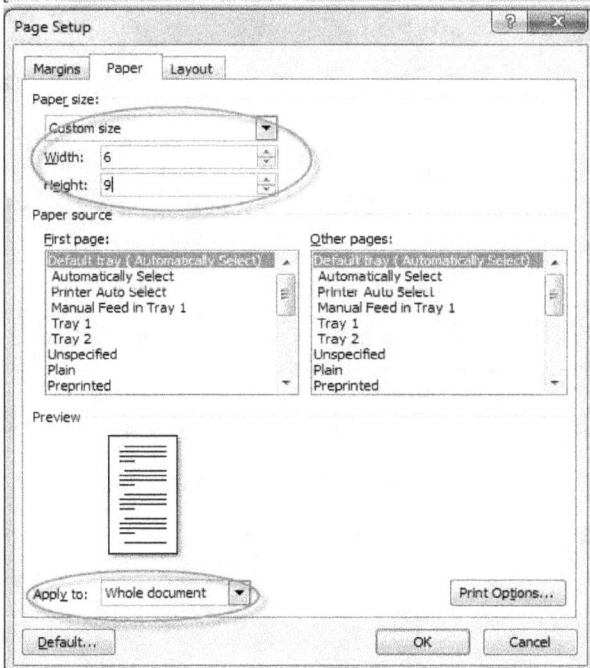

Ensure that your correct width and height are entered.

Page Layout - Size - More paper sizes. Set your width and height based on your book's final trim size. The rest can be left at default unless you have anything fancy to do. Be sure to apply this to the "**Whole document**" prior to proceeding.

A quick note about bleed: Bleed simply means you have elements extending all the way to the edges of a page. If you are submitting your book with any images or elements that bleed, you will add .125" to the width and .25" to the height. For the trim size of 6" x 9" plus bleed, you will size your file at 6.125" x 9.25". Bleed will be further discussed in the Book Cover Layout and Design section of this study guide.

Margins: Simply put, the necessary updates to your margins can be found under Page Layout - Margins - Custom Margins.

Customize your margins based upon the submission requirements for your page count, and whether you are including bleed. For example, for a 152-page book, you will need at least .5" gutter margins.

You will need to format both gutter (inside) margins and outside margins. The outside margins include the top, bottom, and the outside edges of the pages.

Gutter margins: Picture an open book. The gutter margins are the area in the spine/binding region of your open book. These should mirror each other, having the same distance on both sides. You can typically select Mirror Margins in the Multiple Pages area and then set your preferred size for the gutter margins. Remember: the inside margins and gutter margins are the same thing. Set just your gutter margin to eliminate redundancy. The inside margin area can be left at "0".

When reviewing your pages one at a time, remember that the first page is going to appear on the right in your open book. The next will appear on the left, and so on.

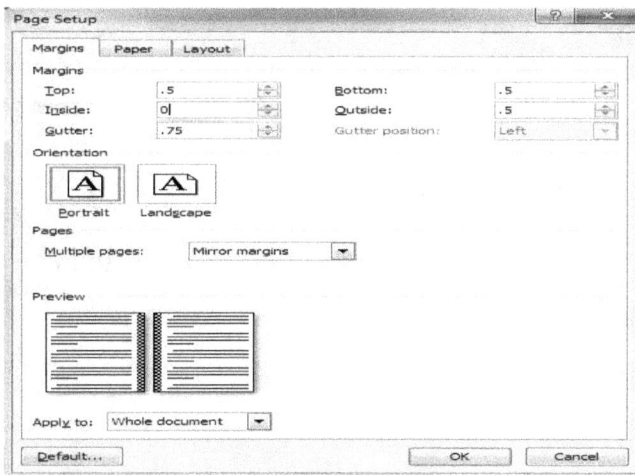

Outside margins: Top, bottom and outside margins will appear more consistent if you keep them the same size. Please review the requirements for your page size, as this will differ slightly if you are including bleed. If you are not including bleed, the requirement is at least .25" for all text, but we recommend .5" so that the text can be easily read.

Recap: Set at least .5" for the top, bottom, and outside

Generally Accepted Gutter Margin Guidelines

24 to 150 pages **.375"**

151 to 300 pages **.5"**

301 to 500 pages **.625"**

501 to 700 pages **.75"**

701 to 828 pages **.875"**

I, Typically, Use .5" for ALL Books up to 300 pages

---

margins. Next to Multiple Pages, select Mirror Margins. Set your gutter margin dependent upon your page count. Setting your gutter margins larger is fine; just don't set them smaller than the requirements below:

DON'T WORRY, A CHEAT SHEET FOR A 6 X 9 INCH BOOK IS INCLUDED AT THE END OF THIS SECTION.

Insert

Now that we've covered the logistics, let's focus on a few aesthetic options. You're going to have to spend time in the Insert tab, at times to include pictures or other graphics into your manuscript.

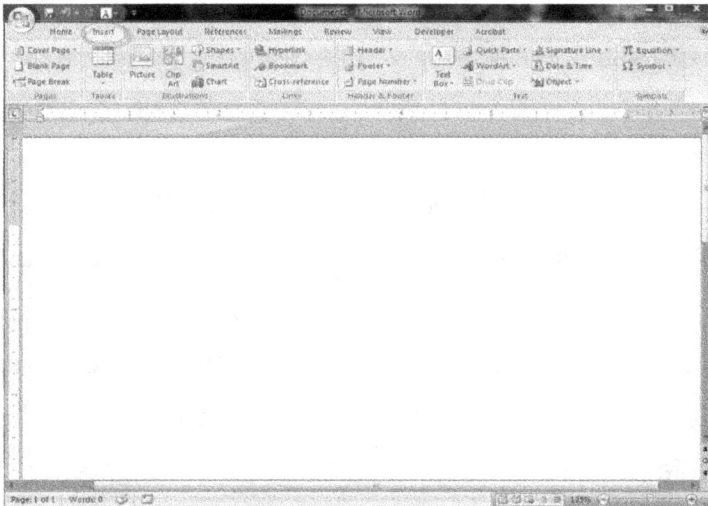

Headers and Drop Caps

If you do not want your header to show on the first page, visit Header - Edit header - and then click on "Different First Page" so that this one stands out. The "Different First Page" preference will fall under the options in this section.

Drop caps: How do you feel about drop caps in a story? If you're a fan, visit Insert - Drop Cap. As a potential note, you will need to have a written paragraph in order to use this action. This is a fun option for the beginning of a new chapter.

A few formatting dos and don'ts for your book:

Return (Enter) key: It is not advised to hit Enter to begin text on a new page. Instead, visit Insert and then Page Break. If you hit the Enter key to begin Chapter 2 on a new page, this formatting will not hold if you later decide to add two new paragraphs to Chapter 1, for example. It is also recommend visiting Page Layout? Breaks to play with the available options. These will typically provide smoother transitions and will result in fewer conversion errors. Of course, you, as the author will eventually determine your own preferences.

With this being said, using the spacing key to advance to the next line is also not advised. The text will flow there naturally as you type. Hitting Enter will bring you to a new line to begin your next paragraph.

Home

Additional aesthetic choices can be made in the Home tab.

Indenting: You can determine your preferred level of indentation under the Home - Paragraph section by looking for these buttons.

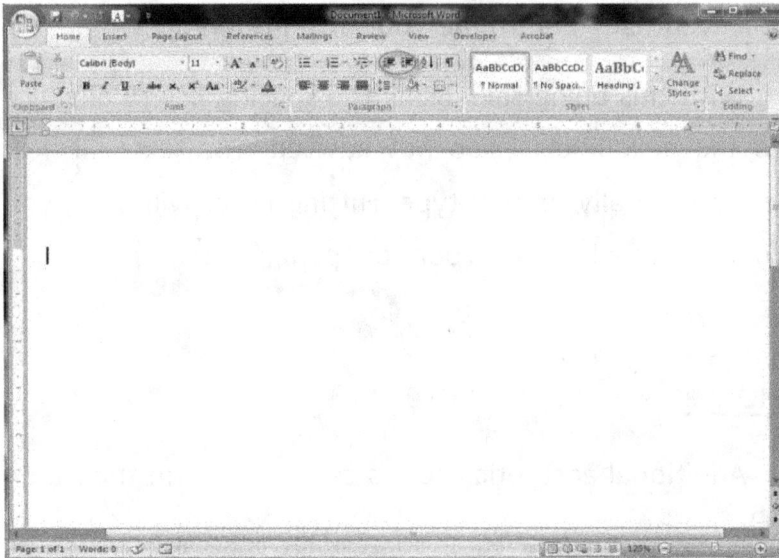

Line spacing: Double-spacing between lines is not necessary. It is more common for a document to be single-spaced. If you must double-space, here's what you should do: in the Home tab, visit the Paragraph section. Next to the centering and justifying options, there will be a section with a blue vertical arrow with 4 lines and a drop-down for you to select your preference.

Paragraph spacing: The line spacing button even allows you to add a space after each paragraph, which is a smart formatting choice as you will likely be taking this action regardless.

Under the Home - Paragraph tab it is also recommend justifying your text. While some prefer to have the text left-justified, we recommend choosing the option that justifies the text on all sides, making each line begin and end in the same position. If you find that the text appears out of alignment when reaching the end of your paragraph hit Enter.

Saving Your File As a PDF

The final hurdle of achieving the file you were envisioning is saving your document as a PDF. The latest versions of Microsoft Word allow a writer to save their finished work in a PDF format. There are also Word to PDF programs available.

Now you can now focus on the nooks and crannies of your story, rather than the intricacies of a complicated program. You are now on your way to accomplishing your creative endeavors.

6 x 9 Inch Book Cheat Sheet

(For Interior Page Layout in Microsoft Word)

_Margins	Paper	Layout
Margins	Paper Size:	Section
Top: 1″ Bottom: 1″	Custom size Width 6	Section start: New page
Left: .65 Right: .65	Height 9	□ Suppress end notes (leave blank)
Gutter .5 Gutter Pos: Left	Paper source	Headers and Footers
Orientation	First page: Other pages:	□√ Different odd and even (check)
Portrait Landscape	Both are Default tray	□ √ Different front page (check)
Pages	Preview	From edge: Header: .2
Multiple pages: Normal	Apply to: Whole document	Footer: .3
		Page
Preview		Vertical alignment: Top
		Preview
Apply to: - Whole document		Apply to: Whole document

6 x 9 Inch Book Cheat Sheet

(For Interior Page Layout in Microsoft Word)

Paragraph	Paragraph
Indents and Spacing	Line and Page Breaks
General	Pagination
Alignment – Justified Outline Level – Body Text	□√ Widow/Orphan control (check this box) □ Keep with next □ Keep lines together □ Page break before (leave next 3 unchecked)
Indentation	
Left – 0 Special Right – 0 First Line – 0.2	Formatting exceptions
Spacing	□ Suppress line numbers □ Don't hyphenate
Before – 0 Line Spacing At After – 6 Multiple - 1.25	Textbox options:
Leave Unchecked	Tight wrap: - None
□ Don't add space between paragraphs of the same style	

If you are at a loss as to where to start in laying out the interior of your 6 x 9 inch book interior, you can use the aforementioned page layout specifications. After you get used to using these functions in Microsoft Word, you can starting making adjustments based on your needs and preferences.

8..

Editing and Grammar

The Process of Writing Your Manuscript

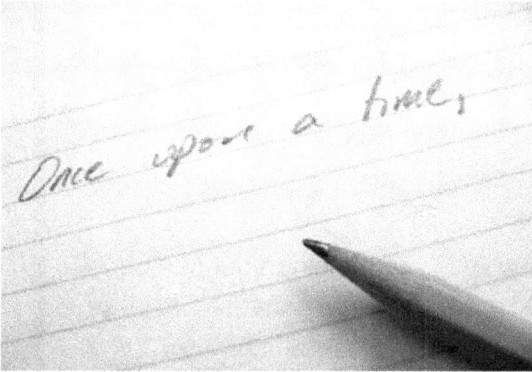

Preparing an outline first, before writing your draft, is recommended.

When writing your draft it is very important to ensure that the following circumstances are fostered:

1. A comfortable environment to ensure productivity.

2. Distractions are minimized while writing.

It should be remembered that almost any type of content can be transformed into a professionally published book.

The trick to writing a successful book is carefully defining your book's audience and then making sure that the content of your book (and later all the marketing for it) targets that same specific audience.

As an author, you are bringing your unique perspective to a subject even if that subject has been written about a thousand times before. Coming up with the perfect book idea that's unique or that offers a new twist on something that's been written about before is an important step in the book writing and publishing process.

Equally important is researching your information and making sure that you have enough interesting and informative content to fill a book. The information then needs to be properly organized so it makes sense and is useful to the reader.

Most successful authors begin the writing process by creating a detailed outline for their book before they actually start researching, writing, and adding visual elements like photos and illustrations.

<u>Editing Your Manuscript</u>

After you have fully written your manuscript draft to your satisfaction, and after you have fully edited your draft, you can then submit your work. Adherence to the following guidelines is required:

1. Your final manuscript should be in Microsoft Word or Open Office format.

2. Be sure to save multiple copies of your work before submitting your manuscript.

3. Along with the manuscript, the following should be submitted:

a. Book Title.

b. Book Subtitle (if applicable).

c. Short, two to ten sentence, description about what book is about (this will go on back book cover).

d. Information about the author (a bio about the author – even if an assumed name is used).

e. A list of all the chapters in the manuscript.

f. Any quality pictures or cover art you wish to use in the book (must be in tiff, jpg, png or format).

g. Bibliographic information (described in following section).

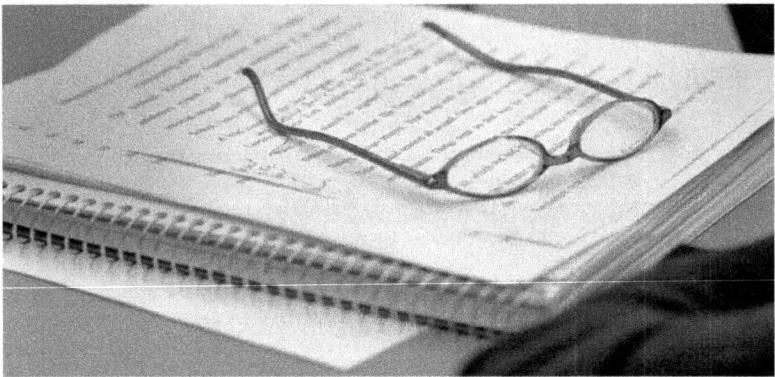

It is essential for a well-written book to contain absolutely no spelling mistakes (that's ALWAYS the goal so that when some inevitable mistakes exist, it won't detract from the book as a whole), grammatical errors, inaccurate information, misprints, or any incorrect details (such as incorrect names, phone numbers, etc.)! In addition to proofreading your writing, you should have your manuscript reviewed by an editor before it goes to press!

A four step manuscript editing process is very advantageous, as follows:

1. Publisher edit after an initial submission

2. Author re-edit

3. Publisher final re-edit, and

4. Author final re-edit

After the manuscript editing process is completed, then the Publisher will copy edit the book which involves the actual layout of the book (this is described in more detail in the following section) and this is then resubmitted to the author for her or his final review. Sometimes manuscript and copy editing are done simultaneously, depending on the circumstances.

It should be noted that manuscript copy editing require a very different skill set than writing a manuscript. Also, many manuscript editors check for spelling, grammatical, and continuity separately.

Copy Editing Your Book

As mentioned previously, copy editing involves the actual layout of the inside of your book. The general layout of a book is as follows:

- ➤ **An Endorsement Page (if necessary)**
- ➤ **Title Page**
- ➤ **Copyright/Publisher Page**
- ➤ **Dedication Page**
- ➤ **Acknowledgement Page**
- ➤ **Table of Contents Page(s)**
- ➤ **Introduction (if necessary)**

After these pages are set up to a certain format and font, then the body of the manuscript work must be laid out in the appropriate fashion. It should be noted that **chapters ALWAYS begin on a right hand page**. There are many other considerations such as page numbering, font format and size, and header language.

After the manuscript and copy editing process has been completed, then the book will be converted into a PDF format (sometimes a Word document is sent, however) for delivery to the requisite online book retailer for sale to the public. Of course you will need an eye-catching book cover and this is described in the following Book Cover Design and Technical Aspects section.

General Lead Times for Publication

Before submission of a manuscript to your indie publishing distributor, it is suggested that the following process occurs:

1) Editing

2) Copy Editing

3) Book Cover creation

4) Book Conversion, then

5) Submission of Book to Online book retailers/distributors

Of course, there are always contingencies. However, if all the processes are completed in a timely fashion, an indie or self-published book should take only two weeks (or even less time), from the date of submission, to be listed for sale on an online retail book site like Amazon.com and Barnes & Noble.com.

Traditional publishing is much more time consuming and it could take over a year, or longer, to get a book published upon submission to a traditional publisher.

Grammar

Proper grammar is vitally essential if an author want to see his or her book noticed for the right reasons. The goal is to try to submit a Perfectly edited manuscript. However, that almost Never happens in real life. However, if a book is properly edited, and any mistakes are far and few in between, the message, instead of the mistakes, shine through!

This book is not intended to teach grammar, but strives to stress the need for a writer to learn all she or he can relating to the proper use of grammar. This is imperative if they want to publish an acceptable manuscript.

Some of the most common mistakes involve the use of quotation marks. So let's review the use of quotation marks.

Quotation Marks

The rules set forth in this section are customary in the United States. Great Britain and other countries in the Commonwealth of Nations are governed by different guidelines.

Rule 1.   **Use double quotation marks to set off a direct (word-for-word) quotation.**

Correct: "When will you be here?" he asked.

Incorrect: He asked "when I would be there."

Rule 2.   **Either quotation marks or italics are customary for titles: magazines, books, plays, films, songs, poems, article titles, chapter titles, etc.**

Rule 3a.   **Periods and commas ALWAYS go inside quotation marks** (This is a very common mistake).

Examples: The sign said, "Walk." Then it said, "Don't Walk," then, "Walk," all within thirty seconds. He yelled, "Hurry up."

Rule 3b.   **Use single quotation marks for quotations within quotations.**

Example: He said, "Dan cried, 'Do not treat me that way.' "

Note that the period goes inside both the single and double quotation marks.

Rule 4.   **As a courtesy, make sure there is visible space at the start or end of a quotation between adjacent single and double quotation marks**. (Your word processing program may do this automatically.)

Not ample space: He said, "Dan cried, 'Do not treat me that way.'"

Ample space: He said, "Dan cried, 'Do not treat me that way.' "

Rule 5a. **Quotation marks are often used with technical terms, terms used in an unusual way, or other expressions that vary from standard usage.**

Examples: It's an oil-extraction method known as "fracking."

He did some "experimenting" in his college days.

I had a visit from my "friend" the tax man.

Rule 5b. **Never use single quotation marks in sentences** like the previous three.

Incorrect: I had a visit from my 'friend' the tax man.

The single quotation marks in the above sentence are intended to send a message to the reader that friend is being used in a special way: in this case, sarcastically. Avoid this invalid usage. Single quotation marks are valid only within a quotation.

Rule 6. **When quoted material runs more than one paragraph, start each new paragraph with opening quotation marks, but do not use closing quotation marks until the end of the passage.**

Example: She wrote: "I don't paint anymore. For a while I thought it was just a phase that I'd get over.

"Now, I don't even try."

Note: The BLUE BOOK of Grammar and Punctuation is an Excellent Resource!

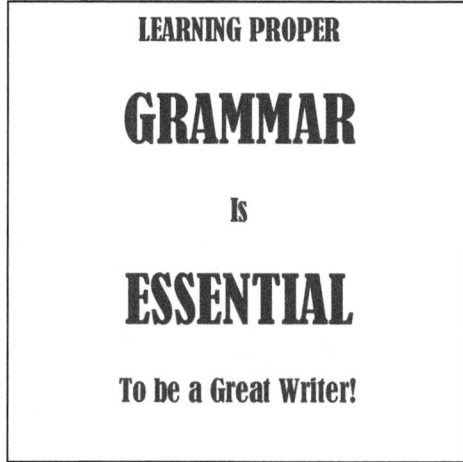

grammar
police

Grammar
Police

*To Serve and
Correct*

LEARNING PROPER

GRAMMAR

Is

ESSENTIAL

To be a Great Writer!

9

Book Cover Design
And Technical Aspects

As an author you can write the greatest prose in the world, but if the cover of your masterpiece is shabby, then many people will look no further than that – a shabby cover. Some covers cost thousands to produce, yet others that are just as intriguing are produced at a much lower cost.

The goal of the author is to produce the most pleasing and professional cover for your book at the most affordable cost.

Some of the requisite information needed to make your book cover includes:

➤ Book Title
➤ Book Sub-title
➤ Endorsements (if required)
➤ Author Information (at least the name of the author)
➤ Byline (a short two or three sentence description of book)
➤ ISBN Bar Coding

Technical Requirements to Make Book Cover

The cover must be submitted as one continuous image and should include a front cover, back cover, and spine, set up for the proper trim size and page count. If only a front cover image is submitted, the printer (like Amazon for example) will attempt to construct a full cover by adding a solid white back cover and spine. If only a back cover and/or spine image is submitted, they will not be able to construct a full cover and the file will be rejected.

Cover Size Requirements

Your cover must, usually, be a single PDF, formatted to the trim size of your book, which includes the back cover, spine, and front cover as one image. You can submit your cover on any size page as long as the printable area is:

Measured exactly to your book's trim size, spine width **plus 0.125" bleed on all sides**, centered horizontally and vertically (see illustrations on page 95).

Calculating the Cover Size

Spine Calculation:

To format your cover you will first want to calculate the spine width of your book. To do so, multiply the total page count with the spine multiplier associated with your book's paper type below:

- For black and white-interior books:

- White paper: multiply page count by 0.002252"

- Cream paper: multiply page count by 0.0025"

- For color-interior books:

- Multiply page count by 0.002347"

Example Calculation:

A 60 page black and white book printed on white paper will be created using the following formula:

60 (pages) x 0.002252" (spine multiplier) = 0.135" (spine width)

Once you have your spine width you can calculate the fully formatted cover size. You will calculate the fully formatted cover size using the spine width calculation, the trim size width and height, and the 0.125" bleed requirement using the following equations:

- Cover Width = Bleed + Back Cover Width + Spine Width + Front Cover Width + Bleed

- Cover Height = Bleed + Trim Height + Bleed

Example Calculation:

6" x 9" trim size with 60 B&W pages on white paper:

Cover Width = 0.125" + 6" + 0.135" + 6" + 0.125" = 12.385"

Cover Height = 0.125" + 9" + 0.125" = 9.25"

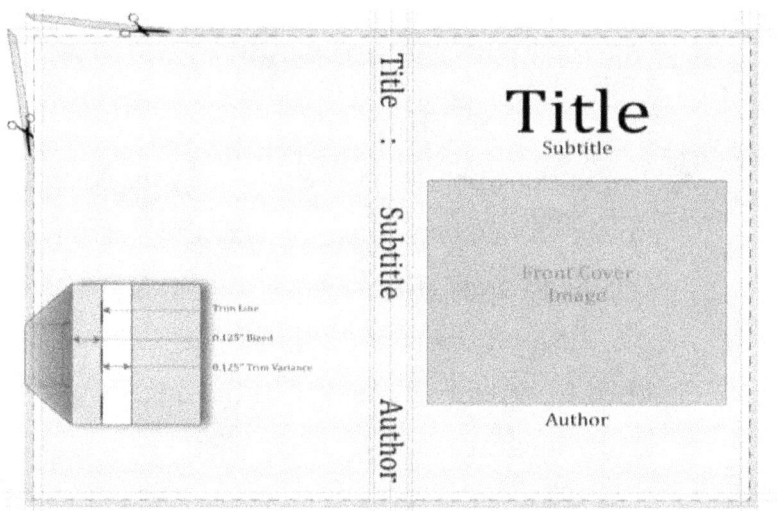

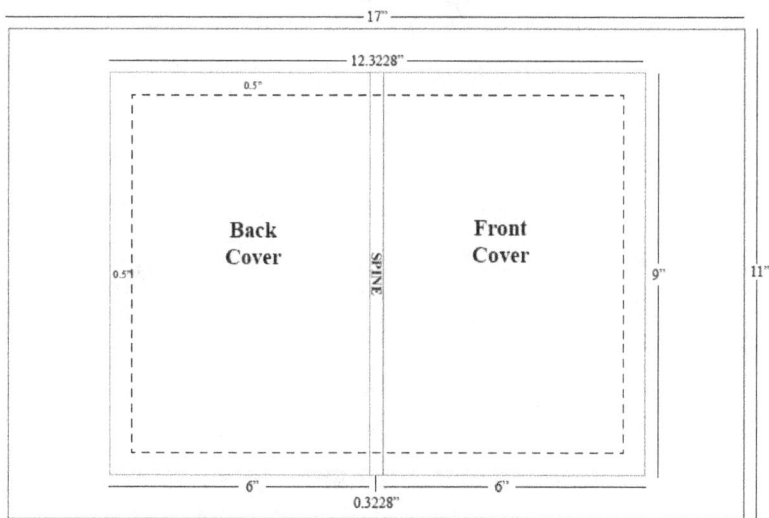

Tips

> It's better to allow more cushion in your design than to crowd the margins. Ideally you'll want at

least .5" between any text and the edge of the page.

➤ The background image or color of your cover image should extend all the way to the edge of the bleed area. (The bleed area should be 0.25" to 0.5" beyond the edge of the image – it does not need to extend all the way to the edge of the 17" x 11" document).

➤ Allow at least 0.5" to .75" vertical cushion on either side of the text on your spine.

➤ To place text on the spine, rotate it so that the left type margin falls at the top of the book. The type will then read correctly from left to right when the book lies front cover up on a horizontal surface.

➤ If you have your own ISBN and barcode, remember to put it on the back cover of your book.

As indicated in the Software Requirements section of this study guide, a strong knowledge of image software, like Photoshop is required to produce quality book covers in-house. Here are some of Uptown's book covers:

10

Book Submission

In this section of the book, we will focus on submission of your written work to **Amazon's Createspace**. The reason, of course, is that amazon is the leading online book retailer and it just makes sense to make your book submissions through them.

A caveat is if you want to print large quantities (for example 50 or more copies) you may want to use Lightning Source, which is the resource used by many publishers that have the distribution network and need to order larger quantities.

Of course, you will need to submit your books to other online outlets like. **Kindle** (an Amazon company) and **Nook** (a Barnes & Noble company).

Once your book is submitted through Amazon, the Kindle submission is easy. At the very end, in the Createspace book submission process, there is a link to the Kindle Direct website.

For submission on Createspace, the following is generally required (this list is not all inclusive):

- ➤ Title Information
    - ▪ Book Title
    - ▪ Subtitle (If applicable)
    - ▪ Primary Author Name
    - ▪ Publication Date
- ➤ ISBN
    - ▪ As a publisher you will be using your own ISBN number purchased directly from R.R. Bowker. Otherwise you could get one from Createspace free, with Createspace being named the publisher (or for a $10 fee for a custom ISBN or $99 to be named as the publisher) if you did not own your own.
- ➤ Interior File
    - ▪ Must be a PDF, Docx, or RTF file that adheres to Createspace's submission guidelines.
- ➤ Cover File
    - ▪ Must be a Full Cover PDF file that adheres to Createspace's submission guidelines.

➤ Distribution

- Choose various distribution channels (like Amazon Europe, Amazon.com etc...)
- Choose the price of your book (there will be listed a minimum price that the book must be priced at or higher).

➤ Description (a subsection of Distribution)

- In the section you will choose categories for the book and input various information about the book including book description, author information, and key words.

➤ Complete Setup

- Submit files for review. A response will be returned within 24 hours of submission.

Nook and Kindle E-Book Submissions

Nook

Nook Press is the e-book division for Barnes and Noble. Nook accepts Microsoft Word, HTML, or TXT files that adhere to submission guidelines.

As to e-book cover images, Nook accepts JPG or PNG files that are at least 750 pixels high and wide and that are no larger than 2 MB large.

Kindle

As stated earlier, the Kindle submission is easy. At the very end, in the Createspace book submission process, there is a link to the Kindle Direct website.

Kindle will accept a Word document or a PDF document (they say Word is the preferred source). They will make the e-book front cover based on the full cover submitted to Createspace.

If you are submitting an e-book directly through **Kindle Direct Publishing**, both JPG and TIFF cover art files are accepted. The artwork must be a minimum of 625 pixels by 1000 pixels (for best quality, the image should be 2500 pixels on the longest side). The cover image cannot be larger than 50 MB. Also, no image larger than 10,000 pixels on the longest side of the image will be accepted.

Getting Your Book Listed on Barnes & Noble.com

Barnes & Noble has a byzantine process for listing a book with them. I won't even both trying to discuss that because you own your own ISBNs purchased from R.R. Bowker.

You are very fortunate because you can avail yourself of ***Bowker Link***, in which you will be able to submit all the required information through their system.

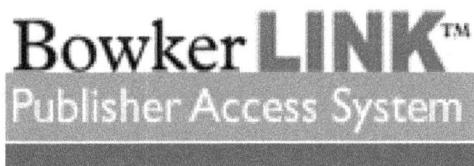

Bowker LINK™
Publisher Access System

Some of the required data for submission on Bower Link is as follows:

- ➢ ISBN
- ➢ Title
- ➢ Author
- ➢ Publisher (or Imprint)
- ➢ Format (paperback or some other format)
- ➢ Price
- ➢ Publication Date
- ➢ BISAC Category Audience
- ➢ BISAC Category Subject

Magically, within a day or two of this submission on Bowker Link, your cover art and all the information you submitted on Createspace (which, of course, appears on Amazon.com) will also appear of Barnes & Noble.com.

Concluding Words

You did it! You have begun your journey to being the owner of your own indie publishing company. You, of course, will have your friends and family to lend support and love.

Write for the love of getting your thoughts out there to others who you may inspire. Write from your experiences and thoughts to benefit others. Stay diligent, but enjoy the process along the way. Good, maybe even great, things will come to you based on your pride and persistence.

Peace Joy & Love

K Kelly

About The Author

At the helm of Uptown Media Joint Ventures, K Kelly is following his passion of helping authors get their viable stories published and marketed to their readers! This passion includes expanding the audiences for recording artists and freelance journalists, as well!

K Kelly is an avid Modern Jazz enthusiast. He proudly owns a vintage collection of over 1000 classic jazz CDs. He authored the book, *Best of the Best Modern Jazz Recordings* which is an effort to compile his significant knowledge of the genre to assist others who want to develop and enjoy their own modern jazz collection.

Start Your Own

INDIE

Publishing

Company!

Everything You Need to Know!

K Kelly McElroy

↑UP TOWN
MEDIA - JOINT VENTURES

Have your book published free of charge!

Forward inquiry to:

info@uptownmediaventures.com

TEAM UPTOWN THANKS YOU FOR YOUR SUPPORT!!!

http://uptownmediaventures.com